Making + MATH + Work

Why Do Math with Letters?

BY JOY VISTO

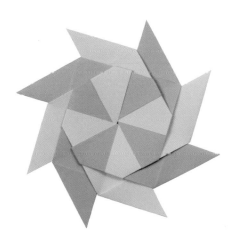

CREATIVE EDUCATION

CREATIVE PAPERBACKS

Published by Creative Education and Creative Paperbacks
P.O. Box 227, Mankato, Minnesota 56002
Creative Education and Creative Paperbacks
are imprints of The Creative Company
www.thecreativecompany.us

Design and production by Liddy Walseth
Art direction by Rita Marshall
Printed in the United States of America

Photographs by Corbis (Corbis, Image Source, Louie Psihoyos), Dreamstime (Photka, Rangizzz), Getty Images (Oliver Brachat, CountryStyle Photography, Cultura/Phil Fisk), iStockphoto (2HotBrazil, hayatikayhan, ivelly, TARIK KIZILKAYA, nattzkamol, Nerthuz, OSTILL, procurator, unalozmen), Shutterstock (ajt, graphixmania, Eduard Kim, Arkady Mazor)

Library of Congress Cataloging-in-Publication Data
Visto, Joy.
Why do math with letters? / Joy Visto.
p. cm. — (Making math work)
Includes bibliographical references and index.
Summary: A helpful guide for understanding the mathematical concepts and real-world applications of algebra, including classroom tips, common terms such as coefficients, and exercises to encourage hands-on practice.
ISBN 978-1-60818-577-1 (hardcover)
ISBN 978-1-62832-178-4 (pbk)
1. Algebra—Juvenile literature. I. Title.

QA155.15.V57 2015
512—dc23 2014034842

CCSS: RI.5.1, 2, 3, 8; RI.6.1, 2, 3, 4, 5, 6, 7; RST.6-8.3, 4, 6, 7

First Edition HC 9 8 7 6 5 4 3 2 1
First Edition PBK 9 8 7 6 5 4 3 2 1

When you think about mathematics, you probably think about a class at school where you do **calculations** and answer word problems. But have you ever thought about math being all around you? It's in every shape and pattern you see. It's in every song you hear. It's in every game you play and any puzzle you solve! The first mathematicians realized this, and they looked for ways to prove it—to show how order and reason could explain much about life as they knew it. Sometimes this was easy to do. But other times, people just didn't get it. Even some of the most intelligent people in history have struggled with math: Albert Einstein once wrote to a child, "Do not worry about your difficulties in Mathematics. I can assure you mine are still greater."

So how can you use whatever you know about math in everyday life? When you *collect* like objects as you clean your room, *distribute* papers to your classmates, or *simplify* a big project into smaller steps, you are using math! In such cases, you are using a type of math known as algebra. This branch of mathematics is concerned with interpreting math sentences so that you can find a specific unknown quantity. *Why do* the letters of algebra work so well with numbers?

Prominent American Series

ALBERT EINSTEIN
MATHEMATICIAN-PHYSICIST
NOBEL PRIZE WINNER
1879–1955

8c

First Day of Issue

Artmaster

THE ART OF
ALGEBRA

ONCE YOU STARTED GETTING THE HANG OF ADDITION, subtraction, multiplication, and division with numbers, your teacher probably threw you a curveball: all of a sudden, there were letters in your homework! If you have never seen such an **equation**, here is an example: 4(3x - 1) = 14. What was your reaction the first time you saw something like that?

MATHEMATICIAN MUHAMMAD IBN MUSA AL-KHWARIZMI ADVANCED ALGEBRAIC STUDY.

You may have thought you were seeing things. Perhaps your teacher had written a crooked plus sign. Maybe you were just confused. Sometimes problems that use variables, which are letters that represent unknown quantities, can look like a strange language. How are you supposed to know what to do with them?

Your teacher would tell you not to worry—there are rules that

$$4(3X-1) = 14$$

help you do this type of math called algebra. Algebra is all about taking a strange-looking equation and manipulating the letters and numbers so that you can determine the value of something that is unknown.

Algebra was developed in the 7th century by Arab mathematicians who were looking to make math work in their lives. Just as ancient Greek mathematicians were drawn to **geometry**, many of the Arabs chose to work more with algebraic concepts because of the strong connections to their everyday work. One such Arab mathematician, Muhammad ibn Musa al-Khwarizmi, made a living out of calculating what people would inherit from relatives who had passed away. This type of work can involve many variables, such as gender, religion, or relationship to the deceased. Al-Khwarizmi became the first person to formalize the process of solving for unknowns.

In 830, al-Khwarizmi used concepts from his work to write a book explaining how to do calculations through balancing equations. This book set up many of the formal rules of working with equations—the very rules you learn in school. Al-Khwarizmi laid out these rules by solving many different equations. The title of his book included the word *al-jabr*, which is the root for the English word "algebra."

Al-Khwarizmi did not use the letter x in his book, though. In fact, he didn't use any variables. Anytime he wanted to represent an unknown quantity, he would write the word *shai*, which is Arabic for "thing." For example, he would have written the previous example problem (4[3x - 1] = 14) as "four times the quantity of one less than three times a thing is equal to fourteen." Which problem looks easier to read and understand? Would you prefer to solve the one with the numbers or the one written out in words?

The notation system of using letters for variables was developed to help make the process of solving equations clearer. However, it took approximately 700 years for this system to appear! After al-Khwarizmi's work was published, it was translated into Latin so that other mathematicians could study it. (At this time, Latin was the universal language used by scholars for their studies.) In Latin, the word for "thing" was translated as *causa* or *cosa*. As it continued to reach other peoples, such as the

SHAI, WHICH IS ARABIC FOR "THING"

THE TWO MIDDLE CELLS AT THE BOTTOM OF THE MAGIC SQUARE GIVE THE DATE: 1514.

Habsburgs in the area we now know as Germany, *cosa* became *coss*.

Such translations gave algebra a nickname in English: "The Cossic Art." Have you ever thought of math as an art form? Artists also find beauty in math. In fact, a 15th-century German artist named Albrecht Dürer included a **magic square** in his engraving *Melencolia I* (above). Likewise, mathematicians find beauty in worked-out solutions as well as in problems that have not yet been solved. In the 16th century, variables were still not a part of the art of algebra. The closest that mathematicians had come to using variables was abbreviating *cosa* and *coss* to "co."

It was not until French scholar François Viète started working with mathematics in the late 16th century that letters began to be used as vari-ables. Viète's job was to **decrypt** secret messages that the French government received. He did math in his spare time. For him, math was a hobby, just like your hobby might be playing basketball or hanging out with friends.

Viète came from a wealthy family, so he was able to take time away from his regular job and publish papers about math. For about six years of his life, he decided to concentrate fully on math. He made many great contributions to mathematics during that time, but his most important involved the introduction of variables. He began his text, *Introduction to the Analytic Art*, by explaining the system he was going to use.

Viète decided to let vowels (the letters a, e, i, o, and u) represent any unknown quantity that he was working with. The remaining letters, the consonants, would represent the known quantities. You may already see some of the problems with that plan. First, a vowel such as the letter *o* cannot be used as a variable because it looks too much like the numeral zero (0). And other vowels are used to represent specific numbers. For instance, the letter *e* is **Euler's number**, equal to approximately 2.718. Similarly, the letter *i* is used in place of the **square root** of negative one, and it's also the basis for a whole set of numbers called the imaginary numbers.

Once Viète's work on variables was published, other mathematicians realized it needed some revisions. Another French mathematician, who was primarily a philosopher, refined Viète's system of variables. René Descartes, working during the

Do unto one side of an EQUATION AS YOU would do unto the other.

early 1600s, decided to use letters from the beginning of the alphabet to represent known quantities, leaving letters at the end of the alphabet to be the unknown quantities. This is the way that variables are still used today.

No matter the notation, the process of working with an algebraic equation is the same. The key to solving an equation is also the same as it has been since al-Khwarizmi first introduced it: both sides of the equation must be balanced. If you have heard of the Golden Rule—do unto others as you would have them do unto you—then you can apply the same idea of balance, or equality, to math. Think of it this way: do unto one side of an equation as you would do unto the other. Every time you add, subtract, multiply, or divide on one side of an equation, you need to do exactly the same operation on the other side.

The idea of making both sides equal has permeated algebra for

hundreds of years. If you can master the process of working with those operations, you will be great at solving equations and finding the value of an unknown. Problems with letters will no longer look like a foreign language, and you will become a talented cossic artist!

Universal Language

By doing math with letters, we are able to treat it as its own language. It's similar to music. Musicians follow a standard system of notation so that they can read and perform pieces written by anyone. By using letters to do math, mathematicians like you can communicate about problems with people from anywhere in the world. Letters as variables, along with common numbers, make math a universal language.

TRANSLATIONS OF THE OPERATIONS

NOW FOR THE REST OF THE WORDS INVOLVED IN MANY ALGEBRA PROBLEMS. You will come across words and phrases that are clues as to which operations are necessary. There are words that represent an unknown quantity, too, such as "a number" and "a value." Therefore, you will need to become a math translator, changing those words into a solvable mathematical **expression** consisting of numbers and variables without an equals sign. In order to get good at doing this, you should familiarize yourself with some math words and what they mean.

On the following pages are the most commonly used operations (addition, subtraction, multiplication, division, and exponents), along with words that are associated with each operation. The final word given in each list describes the result for that operation; often, this word can help translate a phrase.

ADDITION

plus:	five plus a number	5 + x
more than:	five more than a number	x + 5
increased by:	a number increased by 5	x + 5
added to:	a number added to five	5 + x
sum:	the sum of five and a number	5 + x

SUBTRACTION

minus:	five minus a number	5 - x
less:	five less a number	5 - x
decreased by:	a number decreased by 5	x - 5
difference:	the difference of 5 and a number	5 - x

For subtraction, it is important to notice that the order of the **terms** in the operation matters. For example, a number minus 5 (x - 5) is different from 5 minus a number (5 - x). As a result, mathematicians sometimes use the phrase "less than." When you see "less than," the quantity before it is what is being subtracted. For example, "5 less than a number" is x - 5, but "a number less than 5" is 5 - x. Take care to notice the difference between "less" and "less than."

MULTIPLICATION

times:	five times a number	5x
multiplied by:	five multiplied by a number	5x
of:	one-fifth of a number	$\frac{1}{5}x$
product:	the product of five and a number	5x

For multiplication, there are certain words that indicate which product is to be calculated. For example, seeing the word "twice" indicates multiplication by two. A less commonly used word is "thrice," which indicates times three.

DIVISION

divided by:	five divided by a number	5/x
per:	x miles per five hours	x/5
into:	how many times does five go into x	x/5
quotient:	the quotient of a number and five	x/5

EXPONENTS

raised to:	a number raised to the 5th	x^5
powers:	x to the 5th power	x^5

Since an exponent represents repeated multiplication of a number by itself, it might make sense that there are specific names of exponents that can be used to describe a problem, just as there are with multiplication. Problems where a number is raised to the second power may use the word "**squared**," while raising to the third power is shown by "cubed."

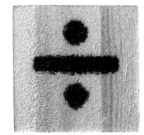

EACH OPERATION IS REPRESENTED BY A DIFFERENT SYMBOL.

In order to translate a problem from written words into a mathematical expression, you need to identify those key words and then change them into their correct operation. Check out the following example, and then try the ones after it.

THE SUM OF A NUMBER AND 11 TIMES THE SAME NUMBER
Underline any words that need to be translated.
   the <u>sum</u> of a <u>number</u> and 11 <u>times</u> the <u>same number</u>
   sum: tells that you will need to be adding
   a number: tells that you need a variable
   times: tells that you will be multiplying
   the same number: tells that you will use the same variable as before
Then change those words into an expression: x + 11x

The letter x is the variable used to represent the unknown number. Notice how 11 is multiplied by x, and then the total is added to make a sum. Following the order of operations process, multiplication comes before addition.

That idea carries over here, as 11 is multiplied first, and then the whole product is used in the sum. Keep that in mind as you try the following problems.

the difference of ten and the product of five and a number

one-tenth of a number which is then increased by three

five less than the quotient of a number and nine

three squared minus a number *

Expressions are only half the story when it comes to algebra. Oftentimes, there are equations that need to be solved. Equations are math sentences that put two expressions together across an equals sign. There is one expression on each side. Just like operations, equals signs have key words, too. Those words include "is," "equal to," and "equals." Using that information as a guide, see if you can translate the following problems.

Three times a number is four less than the same number.

A number is multiplied by three, then six is subtracted to give an answer of nine.

The sum of six times a number and a different number is seven. *

EXPRESSIONS
ARE ONLY
HALF THE STORY
WHEN IT COMES TO ALGEBRA

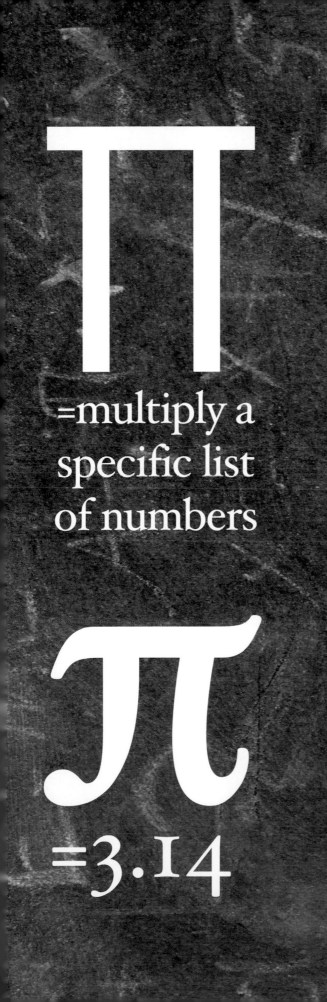

Π
=multiply a specific list of numbers

π
=3.14

As you encounter letters in math, you will find they can serve many purposes. And not all mathematical letters are from the English alphabet! You may know π as representing the number 3.14, but that symbol is also the lowercase version of the Greek letter *pi*. The uppercase letter π tells to multiply a specific list of numbers. While these two may be the same letter (*pi*), they have two different meanings in their different forms.

Pick a variable
THAT HELPS TO
represent that quantity.

In that final question, the phrase "a different number" is used. That should have indicated to you that you needed to pick another variable for your equation. Remember, you can use any variable you want. However, when you are solving a problem with variables, it is important to let people who will be looking at your work know what each variable is representing. To do this, always write a "let" statement, such as "let x = the unknown number." If there is a specific quantity for which you are solving, you can pick a variable that helps to represent that quantity: Let a = the number of apples that Julie has.

The following example shows how you would need to solve for a specific quantity. Begin by writing a let statement to explain the meaning of your variable, and then write an equation. We won't worry about solving it yet!

A stray dog ate 120 pages of your math book. That was ³⁄₁₀ of the total pages of your math book. How many pages were there?

Let p = total pages in the book.

120 = ³⁄₁₀ p

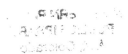

The word "that" refers to the 120 pages, "was" represents equals, and "of" tells that you need to multiply by the total number of pages in the book.

   Set up an equation for each of the following problems. Always begin with a let statement!

There are 160 seventh-graders who need to take a bus to the museum for a field trip. If those students are divided into four buses, how many students will be on each bus? *

Answer Key: Problem C

A baker is making chocolate chip and blueberry muffins. There will be a total of 48 muffins baked. Three times the number of chocolate chip muffins is the number of blueberry muffins. How many blueberry muffins will he make? *

That final problem should have two equations. If you let c = the number of chocolate chip muffins and b = the number of blueberry muffins, the second sentence gives an equation of c + b = 48. The third sentence says that 3c = b.

As you translate the words from a problem, you are setting up a process to find a solution. Be sure to translate carefully and double-check your work—you don't want an early error to throw off the entire solution.

TRANSLATE
THE WORDS
FROM A
PROBLEM

*Answer Key: Problem C

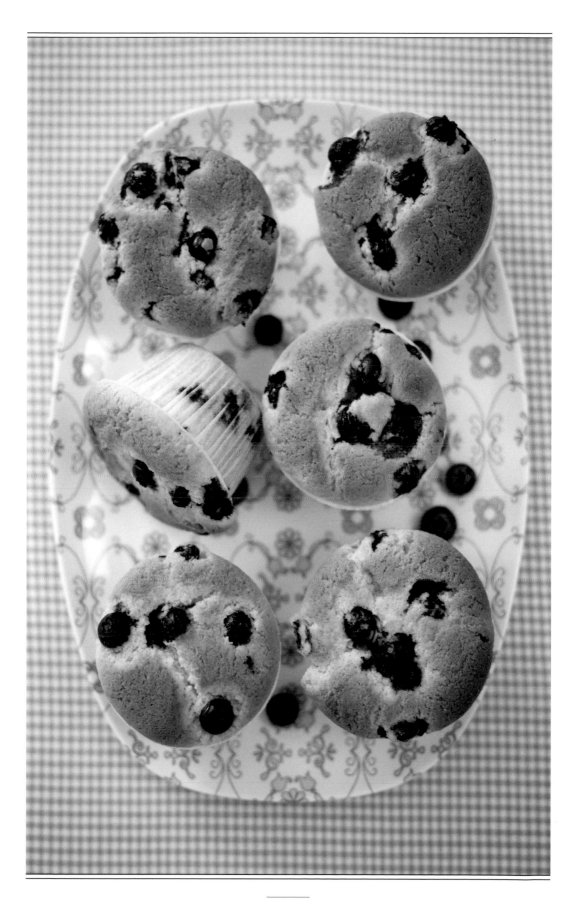

SOLVING WITH THE GOLDEN RULE

BEING ABLE TO WRITE THE NECESSARY EQUATIONS FOR A PROBLEM IS JUST PART OF THE PROCESS. After all, once those equations are written, they need to be solved. There is a process you can follow for every equation you solve. It involves isolating the variable, or getting the variable all by itself on one side of the equation by canceling everything else out. The process presented on the next page uses up to five steps. Those five steps will be laid out in reverse order, moving from easier problems that require fewer steps to more complex problems that need all five.

To understand how to cancel different terms out of an equation, it is important to first know how certain operations are related. Addition and subtraction are opposites. So if you were to add by a specific number and then subtract by the same number, the two would cancel each other out. The same thing happens for multiplication and division.

Because these operations can undo one another, you should always know what operation to do. If you are stuck, read the equation aloud. Listen to yourself say the operation that is happening, and then pick the opposite operation to undo it.

Check out the following example.

$$x + 5 = 6$$

Reading it aloud gives you the statement "x plus five equals six." Since the opposite of plus (addition) is subtraction, you will need to subtract here.

$$x + 5 - 5 = 6 - 5$$

Remember the golden rule for math! If you do an operation on one side of an equation, then do the same to the other side! Simplify the right side. On the left side, the +5 and -5 cancel, and you are left with the value for *x*.

$$x = 1$$

Solve each of the following problems by doing the opposite operation—to both sides.

$x - 4 = 7$ $x + 3 = 10$

$x/4 = 2$ $6x = 42$ *

These types of problems are known as one-step equations because they can be solved in—you guessed it—one step. Two-step equations are slightly more difficult, as they have two steps that must be solved. The final two steps of our five-step process explain how to handle two-step problems. (The first three steps are for more complicated problems and are not used in this case.)

*Answer Key: Problem D

4. Add or subtract to cancel the constant term.

5. Multiply or divide to eliminate the coefficient.

The constant term is the number being added or subtracted that does not have a variable with it. The coefficient is the number that is attached to a variable. In the expression 4x - 3, four is the coefficient and three is the constant term. If there is a variable without a number in front of it, the coefficient of that variable is one. You can write a 1 in there, if it helps you remember that!

Those steps are applied in much the same way as you do the opposite operation for solving a one-step operation. In step four, addition or subtraction is chosen, depending on what operation is happening in the problem. The same is true for multiplication and division in the final step. Predict which operations you would use to solve x/5 + 3 = 7, then check your guess with the solution below.

$$x/5 + 3 = 7$$
$$- 3 \qquad - 3$$
$$x/5 = 4$$

First, subtract three to cancel the constant term. Simplify the right-hand side of the equation as well.

$$x/5 = 4$$
$$\cdot 5 \quad \cdot 5$$
$$x = 20$$

Finish by multiplying by five to cancel the coefficient. Remember that whatever you do to one side, you must do to the other; solve the right-hand side!

Next, solve each of the following two-step equations. Before starting, predict which operations you will need to use, based on what is happening in the problem.

$$3x + 7 = 16 \qquad\qquad x/4 - 6 = -2 \qquad\qquad -5x - 3 = 12 \ ^*$$

Notice that, in each of the above equations, there is only one variable. That will not always be the case. Sometimes a variable will show up on each side of an equation. When that occurs, you need to move all the variables to one side of the equation by completely canceling the variable from one side. The third step in the process helps us handle such a situation. The third step will be done before the final two steps.

3. Move all variables to one side of an equation.

4. Add or subtract to cancel the constant term.

5. Multiply or divide to eliminate the coefficient.

In order to move variables across an equals sign, you need to do the opposite operation of the variable. If the variable is being subtracted or has a negative coefficient, then add that quantity to the other side. If the variable is being added or has a positive coefficient, subtract. Look at the following terms; decide if you should add or subtract to cancel them.

$$4x \qquad\qquad -5x \qquad\qquad x \qquad\qquad -2x \ ^*$$

When you are adding or subtracting with variables, remember that they can be subtracted only from other terms that have variables. Think of it as working with apples and oranges. You can subtract 4 apples from 10 apples, but you cannot subtract 4 apples from 10 oranges—there aren't any apples to start with! The same is true for terms that have an x. You can take away $4x$ from $10x$, but you cannot subtract 4x from 10. Do the following operations. As

*Answer Key: Problem E   *Answer Key: Problem F

you go along, remember to subtract only the coefficients. When you take 4 apples from 10 apples, you are left with 6 apples. If you subtract 4x from 10x, the difference (6x) should have an *x* in it!

4x - 2x   **7x + 5x**   **11x + 4x**   **3x - 5x** [*]

If you can do those operations easily, you will be able to solve equations where there are variables on both sides. There is an example of such a problem below. In this problem, the steps are numbered to match up with the steps in our process.

$$5x + 7 = 3x + 15$$
$$-3x \qquad -3x$$
$$2x + 7 = 15$$

3. Move all the variables to one side by subtracting 3x. When you find the difference of each side, remember to keep *x* in your answer on the left side. On the right side, it has been eliminated.

*Answer Key: Problem G

$$2x + 7 = 15$$
$$\underline{-7 \quad -7}$$
$$2x \quad = 8$$

4. Cancel the constant term by subtracting 7. Simplify again.

$$2x \quad = 8$$
$$\div 2 \quad \div 2$$
$$x \quad = 4$$

5. Eliminate the coefficient through division. Solve the problem!

Try the following problems on your own. Be careful with the x terms. Make sure that you don't lose the x when you add or subtract those variable terms.

$-3x + 6 = -7x + 18$ $\qquad$ $5x - 8 = 14x + 28$ $\qquad$ $6x + 7 = 4x + 19$ *

As you were figuring out those problems, how did you decide which variable term to move? Often, it is easiest to move the variable so that the resulting coefficient is positive. It took mathematicians hundreds of years to accept that negative numbers worked for math. It's okay if you are still struggling with them. You can make it easier on yourself if your final division is with a positive number.

The final answer will not depend on which variable you move first. Maybe you're used to always getting the variable on the left side of the equation. However, you can solve equations with the variable on the right side as well. Look at the examples on the next page to see how that is true. In both problems, $-4x + 6 = x - 14$ is being solved for x. In the first example, x is subtracted from both sides to isolate the variable on the left side of the equation. In the second example, $4x$ is added to both sides. The variable ends up on the right, but there are fewer negative numbers to deal with.

Answer Key: Problem H

Example 1:

$$-4x + 6 = x - 14$$
$$ -x \quad -x$$
$$-5x + 6 = -14$$
$$ -6 \quad -6$$
$$-5x = -20$$
$$\div -5 \quad \div -5$$
$$x = 4$$

Example 2:

$$-4x + 6 = x - 14$$
$$+4x +4x$$
$$6 = 5x - 14$$
$$+14 +14$$
$$20 = 5x$$
$$\div 5 \quad \div 5$$
$$4 = x$$

Did you notice how the two problems gave the same answer, but the operations in the second example were much easier to perform? If you can recognize how to make working with the variables easier, it will help you become a better solver. This is not something that you can master right away, but as you practice doing more problems, you will start to recognize when to add and when to subtract the variables.

These first three steps work with solving equations by using math's Golden Rule. All the operations that were used involved moving terms and quantities across the equals sign by doing the opposite operations. Sometimes, though, there is work that needs to happen on the same side of an equals sign before you can take a problem all the way to its conclusion.

Recognize how to MAKE WORKING WITH *the variables easier*

Exponential Problems

The exponent on the variables has been a one up to this point. As a result, we have had only one answer to each problem. According to the Fundamental Theorem of Algebra, for any exponent, n, an equation will have n solutions. Although this theorem does not deal solely with algebra, it does reference this main idea: whenever you are solving an equation, you should have as many solutions as the largest exponent in the problem.

THE FULL PROCESS

IN ORDER FOR YOU TO BE ABLE TO SOLVE MORE PROBLEMS LIKE THE ONES YOU JUST ENCOUNTERED, the equation must be set up in a particular format. In every problem you've tackled so far, each side of the equation has had at most two terms. There was a term with an x variable and a constant term. In an equation like that, all the like terms on each side of the equals sign have been collected together. Before you can start moving things across the equals sign, this type of simplification must be done. The first two steps of the solution process involve setting up the two sides of the equals sign. We will examine the second step to start.

2. Collect like terms.
3. Move all variables to one side of an equation.
4. Add or subtract to cancel the constant term.
5. Multiply or divide to eliminate the coefficient.

Like terms are terms that have the same variables raised to the same exponents. Examples of like terms are x and 4x, y^2 and $6y^2$, or $4x^2y^3$ and $5x^2y^3$. In that final example, the *x* part of each term has an exponent of two and the *y* part has an exponent of three. Constant terms are always like terms. In the list below, there are three pairs of like terms. Can you identify all three pairs?

$4x^2$ $5x^2\,y^2$ 5 $3x^2$ 17 $x^2\,y^2$ *

Now the like terms can be collected, or grouped together. By collecting the like terms, you are simplifying the side of the equation so that it looks like the equations that you previously solved. Remember when you were moving all the variables to one side in a previous example? That resulted in a like term, too.

When you collect like terms, the answer should be another like term. Collect the like terms from the pairs you collected previously. Remember that the coefficient of x^2y^2 is one. Your answers will be $7x^2$, $5x^2y^2$, and 22. Notice how the answer from $4x^2$ and $3x^2$ had an x^2. The exponents do not change. Think of math terms as different fruits. The terms $4x^2$ and $3x^2$ can be thought of as four apples and three apples. When you put those apples together, you get more apples. They don't all of a sudden become oranges! The exponent on the original term was two, so the answer will have the same exponent. Take a look at the following example problem before tackling the ones below it.

*Answer Key: Problem I

$$4x + 7x + 6 = 3x + 22$$

$11x + 6 = 3x + 22$ **2. Collect 4x and 7x to get 11x.**

$- 3x \quad\quad - 3x$ **3. Move all the variables to one side, subtracting 3x.**

$8x + 6 = 22$ **Simplify. Just do 11 - 3. Keep the _x_!**

$\quad\quad -6 \;\; -6$ **4. Subtract six to cancel the constant term.**

$8x = 16$ **Simplify.**

$÷ 8 \; ÷ 8$ **5. Divide to eliminate the coefficient.**

$x = 2$ **Finish solving!**

Everything after the first step was the same as what you had already practiced. In the problems below, collect the like terms and then finish solving.

$$5x - 2x - 9 = 6x - 3 \quad\quad\quad 4x + 3x + 2x + 17 = 6x + 26$$

$$6x - 8 = 2x + 2x + 16 \text{ *}$$

Every time you add another step to the process, there is an opportunity to make small mistakes. See if you can spot the mistakes in the two problems below. Two students were solving the same equation, and they got different answers. Help them find out whose answer is correct!

Student A: $x + x - 6 = 6x + 22$ **Student B:** $x + x - 6 = 6x + 22$

            $8x = 16$ $2x - 6 = 6x + 22$

            $÷8 \;\; ÷8$ $-2x \quad\quad -2x$

            $x = 2$ $-6 = 4x + 22$

                                              $- 22 \quad\quad - 22$

                                              $-28 = 4x$

                                              $÷ 4 \;\; ÷ 4$

                                              $-7 = x$

*Answer Key: Problem J

Orderly Lines

Equations containing both x and y have a slightly different solution: a line. A specific value for x, when substituted into the solved equation, will give an answer for y. Those two values for x and y represent an ordered pair, which can be plotted on a graph. Generating infinitely many ordered pairs creates a line. This idea of equations becoming lines led to a new branch of mathematics called algebraic geometry.

If you are stuck, perhaps it would be helpful to remember that like terms can be collected only on one side of the equals sign. In her work, Student A put together all the x terms from the equation on one side and all the constant terms on another side. If there are two x terms on one side of an equals sign and 6x on the other side, then they are not alike. You cannot collect terms that are on different sides of an equation. This is important to remember.

Before any of these other steps can occur, though, there is one step that will set everything in motion. It involves simplifying the two sides of the equals sign. Anytime you see any grouping symbols, usually parentheses, you need to use the **distributive property** to remove them. The word "distribute" means to pass out shares of something. When a number is outside parentheses, it needs to be passed out to all the terms inside the parentheses. To distribute that number, multiply it by each of the terms inside the parentheses. The distributive property is therefore the first step of the solving process.

1. **Use the distributive property to remove grouping symbols.**
2. **Collect like terms.**
3. **Move all variables to one side of an equation.**
4. **Add or subtract to cancel the constant term.**
5. **Multiply or divide to eliminate the coefficient.**

Use the distributive property to simplify the following expressions.

$4(3x + 2)$ $-3(7x - 2)$ $9(8x + 10)$ *

To see the distributive property in action, check out the example opposite. It makes use of all five steps of the process to solve for x.

Answer Key: Problem K

6(3x - 2) + 4 = 9x + 10	**1. Use the distributive property.**
18x - 12 + 4 = 9x + 10	**2. Collect like terms.**
18x - 8 = 9x + 10	**3. Move all the variables to one side.**
9x - 8 = 10	**4. Cancel the constant term.**
9x = 18	**5. Eliminate the coefficient.**
x = 2	

Now try some problems on your own. As you are going through, keep a mental checklist of each step that you complete. If you don't need to do a specific step, then you may skip over that one.

$$-2(x + 4) + 5x = x + 4 \qquad 5(x + 2) + 8 = 7x - 12$$
$$3(x + 2) + 4x = 10x \ *$$

The five-step solving process will help you solve any problem that requires isolating a specific variable. It's especially useful when there is both an *x* term and a *y* term in the equation. Just remember that if two things are not like terms, they cannot be mixed. Check out the following example. In this problem, the equation is being solved for *y*.

2(4x + y) - 3x = 7x + 10	**1. Use the distributive property.**
8x + 2y - 3x = 7x + 10	**2. Collect like terms.**
5x + 2y = 7x + 10	
2y = 2x + 10	**3. Move like variables to one side.**
y = x + 5	**5. Divide to eliminate the coefficient.**

As you may have noticed, the final division involved all the terms. In the problem above, everything was divided by two: 2y ÷ 2 = y, 2x ÷ 2 = x, and 10 ÷ 2 = 5. Just as you add or subtract only with coefficients when collecting like terms, you divide the coefficients without changing any variables.

*Answer Key: Problem L

Solve each of the following problems for *y* to get more practice with this concept.

$3(y - 6) + 4x = 16x$ $7y = 5(x - 7) + 2y$ $-2y = 6(x - 1) -10$ *

   If you can master these five steps and store them in your brain, you will be able to solve anything! So much of math involves finding a solution; it even carries into your science classes. Knowing how to solve any type of problem, for any particular variable, will be beneficial to you now and later in life. Thanks to letters, doing algebra today is much neater and makes a lot more sense. Instead of using words to describe the entire problem, we can just use letters!

*Answer Key: Problem M

MATH TOOLKIT

1. You may have learned to write your multiplication problems using × to represent that operation. However, as you start to use *x* as a variable in your problems, you will encounter some difficulties with that notation. As a result, mathematicians rarely use × to show multiplication. Instead, they may use parentheses or a dot. For example, five times seven can be written as (5)(7) or $5 \cdot 7$. Familiarize yourself with the various ways multiplication can be shown!

2. Word problems can hide a lot of information. Some strategies for finding the clues include reading the problem aloud, circling any numbers and their units, underlining descriptions, and putting a box around what the problem is asking you to do. Here's an example of what this would look like:

A seventh-grader has 41 basketball cards. If he gets 17 more, he will have exactly twice as many as his friend. How many does his friend have?

Once you've isolated the information, you should be able to find the answer quickly. Do this for every word problem!

3. As you are solving equations, it may be helpful for you to draw a vertical line through the equals sign to split the equation into its two sides. Any operation that happens on one side must happen on the other. Showing your work by writing in the operation that you are doing on each side of that line helps you to track your progress and know that you are always keeping your equation balanced.

4. A problem may look done once the variable is isolated from the final answer. But there's one more thing: Go back and substitute that number for the variable, plugging it in every time the variable appears. You can then use PEMDAS (the order of operations) to simplify each side of the equals sign. If you did the problem correctly, the two sides should be equal! You can now be 100 percent sure that you have the right answer.

GLOSSARY

calculations: operations performed on numbers

decrypt: undo a code applied to a word or phrase so that it can be read

distributive property: a property which says that numbers can be distributed into a group of parentheses by multiplying each inside term by that outside number

equation: a math sentence that connects two equal expressions

Euler's number: equal to approximately 2.718, this number is calculated by adding up fractions where the denominator increases by multiplication of the next largest whole number (1/1 + 1/(1·2) + 1/(1·2·3) + 1/(1·2·3·4) + ...)

expression: a mathematical phrase made up of numbers, variables, and any operations

geometry: a branch of mathematics that works with the properties of shapes

magic square: a mathematical problem where numbers are filled into a square grid so that the horizontal, vertical, and diagonal lines all add up to the same number

square root: a number that when multiplied by itself gives back an original number; for example, three is the square root of nine, three times three is nine

squared: multiplied a number by itself; represented with an exponent of two

terms: numbers or variables that are being added or subtracted in an equation

SELECTED BIBLIOGRAPHY

Berlinghoff, William P., and Fernando Q. Gouvêa. *Math through the Ages: A Gentle History for Teachers and Others.* Washington, D.C.: MAA Service Center, 2004.

Macbeth, Danielle. "Viète, Descartes, and the Emergence of Modern Mathematics." *Graduate Faculty Philosophy Journal*, vol. 2, no. 25 (2004): 87–117.

O'Connor, John J., and Edmund F. Robertson. "History Topics: Algebra Index." MacTutor History of Mathematics Archive. http://www.history .mcs.st-and.ac.uk/Indexes/Algebra.html.

Rooney, Anne. *The Story of Mathematics.* London: Arcturus, 2008.

Struik, Dirk J. *A Concise History of Mathematics.* New York: Dover, 1987.

Wingard-Nelson, Rebecca. *Problem Solving and Word Problems.* Berkeley Heights, N.J.: Enslow, 2004.

WEBSITES

Algebra Lessons at Coolmath.com
http://coolmath.com/algebra/06-solving-equations/index.html
Find out more about solving linear equations, including some extra practice problems.

Math Is Fun: Like Terms
http://www.mathsisfun.com/algebra/like-terms.html
This page explains how to collect like terms and features more practice problems.

Note: Every effort has been made to ensure that the websites listed above are suitable for children, that they have educational value, and that they contain no inappropriate material. However, because of the nature of the Internet, it is impossible to guarantee that these sites will remain active indefinitely or that their contents will not be altered.

INDEX

ANSWER KEY

Problem A

the <u>difference</u> of ten and the <u>product of</u> five and <u>a number:</u> 10 - 5x

<u>one-tenth of a number</u> which is then <u>increased by</u> three: ⅒ x + 3

five <u>less than</u> the <u>quotient</u> of <u>a number</u> and nine: x/9 - 5

three <u>squared minus a number</u>: 3^2 - x

Problem B

Three <u>times a number</u> is four <u>less than</u> the <u>same number</u>: 3x = x - 4

<u>A number</u> is <u>multiplied by</u> three, then six is <u>subtracted</u> to <u>give an answer</u> of nine: x · 3 - 6 = 9

The <u>sum</u> of six <u>times a number</u> and a <u>different number is</u> seven: 6 · x + y = 7

Problem C

There are 160 seventh-graders who need to take a bus to the museum for a field trip. If those students are <u>divided into</u> four buses, how many students will be on each bus?

Let s = students on each bus.

s = ¹⁶⁰⁄₄

A baker is making chocolate chip and blueberry muffins. There will be a total of 48 muffins baked. Three times the <u>number of chocolate chip</u> muffins <u>is</u> the <u>number of blueberry</u> muffins. How many blueberry muffins will he make?

Let c = chocolate chip muffins, b = blueberry muffins.

c + b = 48

3c = b

Problem D

x - 4 = 7, add four to both sides, x = 11

x + 3 = 10, subtract three from both sides, x = 7

x/4 = 2, multiply both sides by four, x = 8

6x = 42, divide both sides by six, x = 7

Problem E

3x + 7 = 16

3x = 9

x = 3

x/4 - 6 = -2

x/4 = 4

x = 16

-5x - 3 = 12

-5x = 15

x = -3

Problem F

4x: subtract 4x from each side

-5x: add 5x to cancel

x: subtract x from each side

-2x: add 2x to cancel

Problem G

4x - 2x = 2x

7x + 5x = 12x

11x + 4x = 15x

3x - 5x = -2x

Problem H

-3x + 6 = -7x + 18

4x + 6 = 18

4x = 12

x = 3

5x - 8 = 14x + 28
-8 = 9x + 28
-36 = 9x
-4 = x

6x + 7 = 4x + 19
2x + 7 = 19
2x = 12
x = 6

Problem I

$4x^2$ and $3x^2$

$5x^2 y^2$ and $x^2 y^2$

5 and 17

Problem J

5x - 2x - 9 = 6x - 3
3x - 9 = 6x - 3
-9 = 3x - 3
-6 = 3x
-2 = x

4x + 3x + 2x + 17 = 6x + 26
9x + 17 = 6x + 26
3x + 17 = 26
3x = 9
x = 3

6x - 8 = 2x + 2x + 16
6x - 8 = 4x + 16
2x - 8 = 16
2x = 24
x = 12

Problem K

4 · 3x + 4 · 2 = 12x + 8
-3 · 7x + -3 · -2 = -21x + 6
9 · 8x + 9 · 10 = 72x + 90

Problem L

$-2(x + 4) + 5x = x + 4$

$-2x - 8 + 5x = x + 4$

$3x - 8 = x + 4$

$2x - 8 = 4$

$2x = 12$

$x = 6$

$5(x + 2) = 7x - 12$

$5x + 10 = 7x - 12$

$10 = 2x - 12$

$22 = 2x$

$11 = x$

$3(x + 2) + 4x = 10x$

$3x + 6 + 4x = 10x$

$7x + 6 = 10x$

$6 = 3x$

$2 = x$

Problem M

$3(y - 6) + 4x = 16x$

$3y - 18 + 4x = 16x$

$3y - 18 = 12x$

$3y = 12x + 18$

$y = 4x + 6$

$7y = 5(x - 7) + 2y$

$7y = 5x - 35 + 2y$

$5y = 5x - 35$

$y = x - 7$

$-2y = 6(x - 1) - 10$

$-2y = 6x - 6 - 10$

$-2y = 6x - 16$

$y = -3x + 8$

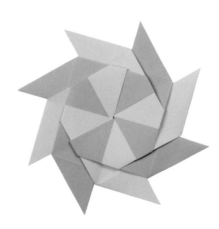